D1172941

SandCastle™

Animal Sounds

FROGS CROAK!

Pam Scheunemann

Consulting Editor, Diane Craig, M.A./Reading Specialist

A Division of ABDO

ABDO
Publishing Company

visit us at www.abdopublishing.com

Published by ABDO Publishing Company, a division of ABDO, P.O. Box 398166, Minneapolis, Minnesota 55439. Copyright © 2011 by Abdo Consulting Group, Inc. International copyrights reserved in all countries. No part of this book may be reproduced in any form without written permission from the publisher. SandCastle™ is a trademark and logo of ABDO Publishing Company.

Printed in the United States of America, North Mankato, Minnesota
102010
012011

 PRINTED ON RECYCLED PAPER

Editor: Liz Salzmann
Content Developer: Nancy Tuminelly
Cover and Interior Design and Production: Oona Gaarder-Juntti, Mighty Media, Inc.

Photo Credits: James Bettaso, Shutterstock

Library of Congress Cataloging-in-Publication Data
Scheunemann, Pam, 1955-
  Frogs croak! / Pam Scheunemann.
    p. cm. -- (Animal sounds)
  ISBN 978-1-61613-572-0
  1. Frogs--Vocalization--Juvenile literature. I. Title.
  QL668.E2S288 2011
  597.8'91594--dc22
                                   2010018731

SandCastle™ Level: Transitional

SandCastle™ books are created by a team of professional educators, reading specialists, and content developers around five essential components—phonemic awareness, phonics, vocabulary, text comprehension, and fluency—to assist young readers as they develop reading skills and strategies and increase their general knowledge. All books are written, reviewed, and leveled for guided reading, early reading intervention, and Accelerated Reader® programs for use in shared, guided, and independent reading and writing activities to support a balanced approach to literacy instruction. The SandCastle™ series has four levels that correspond to early literacy development. The levels are provided to help teachers and parents select appropriate books for young readers.

Emerging Readers
(no flags)

Beginning Readers
(1 flag)

Transitional Readers
(2 flags)

Fluent Readers
(3 flags)

contents

FROGS

Frogs live here. Frogs live there. Frogs live almost everywhere!

3

Not every frog can make a noise.

Some types of frogs do not have the body parts needed to make sounds.

And when they do, it's just the boys.

Male frogs croak to attract female frogs. Only a few types of female frogs croak back.

Each type of frog has its own sound.

Some frogs that look the same can only be told apart by the sounds they make.

By their croaks they know if friends are around!

Frogs will fight with strange frogs. They can tell from another frog's croak whether it is a friend.

Watch out for frogs that are very bright.

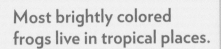

Most brightly colored frogs live in tropical places.

Their poison keeps predators from taking a bite!

Very bright colors tell predators that the frog is poisonous.

Some frogs hide well among the leaves.

Predators have a hard time finding frogs that blend in with their surroundings.

Others spend their
lives high up in trees.

Tree frogs have sticky pads on their feet. The pads help them hold onto branches.

A frog's croak can
be soft or loud.

Frogs puff up with air when they croak. The air makes the croaking louder.

When a frog croaks, it is very proud!

Glossary

attract (p. 6) – to cause someone or something to come near.

blend (p. 17) – to match the surrounding environment.

female (p. 6) – being of the sex that can produce eggs or give birth. Mothers are female.

male (p. 6) – being of the sex that can father offspring. Fathers are male.

pad (p. 19) – a soft, thick area on the bottom of an animal's toe or foot.

poisonous (p. 15) – containing a substance that can injure or kill.

surroundings (p. 17) – the conditions and things around something or someone.

tropical (p. 13) – located in the hottest areas on earth.

Frog Around the World

English - frog

French - grenouille

German - frosch

Japanese - kaeru

Spanish - rana

Swedish - groda

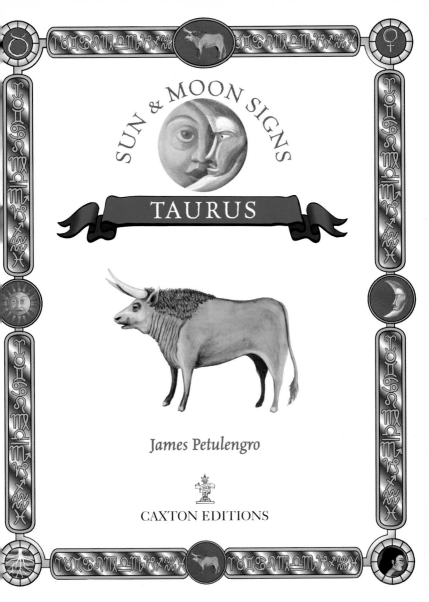

SUN & MOON SIGNS

TAURUS

James Petulengro

CAXTON EDITIONS

TAURUS
CONTENTS